THE WINE AND WISDOM SERIES No.4

MIXED DOUBLES

A One Act Play

Lynn Brittney

GW00632321

PERFORMING ARTS SERVICE
ESSEX

Published by Playstage
United Kingdom.

An imprint of Write Publications Ltd

www.playsforadults.com

Designed by Kate Lowe, Greensands Graphics
Printed by Creeds Ltd, Bridport, Dorset

Note to producers about staging "Mixed Doubles"

The action of the play takes place in a tennis club, so therefore any set dressing, such as a notice board etc. should reflect that fact.

The stage should be set out as for a quiz night with several small tables and chairs (approximately four to a table). The quizmaster and his wife should be upstage centre with two chairs, a small table and a flip chart on an easel.

It is important that the actors behave as though it were a quiz night and when they are not speaking they are miming activity (heads huddled together; drinking; eating; writing etc.) so that there is a constant appearance of movement.

The supposed entrance from the car park can be either stage left or right and the entrance to the kitchen should be on the opposite side.

It is important that the pace of dialogue is kept up in this piece, otherwise it will flag.

There is a break in the centre of the play, signifying a passage of time. This is achieved by a brief blackout with music and, when the lights come on, the meal has finished. This could be done by the actors having used paper plates, crumpled serviettes, left-over pieces of French bread and so on, in their bags, which they produce and place in front of them during the blackout.

Groups performing this piece may find that it is slightly too long to meet the time requirements of a One Act Play Festival but that it is perfect as half of a one act double bill for their regular audiences.

WINE AND WISDOM 4 : MIXED DOUBLES

CAST (In order of appearance)

GEORGE	meticulous and fussy, running quizzes is his hobby, age 50+
HEATHER	George's wife, rather a nervous and passive woman, age 50+
MARJORIE	bossy woman, serves on lots of committees, age 50+
ERIC	Marjorie's husband, good-natured but hen-pecked, age 50+
TRACY	flashy and flirty, aged 30+
MIKE	Tracy's husband, surly ageing rocker, age 50+
SHELAGH	pleasant and motherly, age 60+
DONALD	Shelagh's husband, humorous, age 60+
MARTIN	pedantic know-it-all, irritating, age 40+
ALICE	long-suffering wife to Martin, age 40+
REBECCA	bored teenager, age 14 (could be slightly older)
PAT	sensible and firm former teacher, age 60+
SALLY	Pat's granddaughter, classmate of Rebecca's

8 female and 5 male parts.

The action takes place at a local tennis club.

WINE AND WISDOM 4
MIXED DOUBLES
SCENE 1

The setting is a quiz night held by a local tennis club. There are four tables set out - each with four chairs around them. There is a top table for the quizmaster and his assistant, with two chairs, and to one side is a flipchart with a large score sheet drawn out on it. The names of the teams have not yet been added in. As the scene opens, GEORGE, the quizmaster, and his wife, HEATHER, are bustling about getting things ready. GEORGE sets up a CD player and plugs it into an extension lead. GEORGE is a very meticulous and rather domineering man, who loves to be the centre of attention. His wife is rather nervous and passive.

GEORGE	Did you bring the Jokers?
HEATHER	What?
GEORGE	The Jokers? Did you bring them?
HEATHER	Oh God! Did I? Did you put them in my bag?
GEORGE	*(testily)* I never took them *out* of your bag after the Probus Club quiz. If *you* haven't taken them out then they are still in there.
HEATHER	I'll look. *(She rifles through a large bag)*
GEORGE	*(patronisingly)* I'd have thought that we do this often enough dear, for you to have everything at your fingertips.

HEATHER	I have. That's not fair George. I'm always organised.
GEORGE	*(accusingly)* Not just lately you haven't been. I don't know what's the matter with you lately. You don't seem to be paying attention half the time.
HEATHER	Sorry.
GEORGE	How many are we expecting tonight anyway?
HEATHER	Oh the usual crowd I think. Marjorie said that she and Eric were making up a team with the Mackenzies...um...Tracy and Mike are coming with Alice and Martin...
GEORGE	*(dismayed)* Oh no ! Not Mr Know it All!
HEATHER	Oh he's not that bad George. He can't help being very knowledgeable. It's all those crosswords he does.
GEORGE	*(irritable)* He can help being so bloody pompous though. That's ruined my evening now. I wouldn't have agreed to do this if I'd have known that Martin was coming.
HEATHER	Oh don't be silly George. One person can't make that much difference.
GEORGE	Oh really? Well just let him challenge one of my answers, that's all, and I shall lose my temper.
HEATHER	*(anxious)* Oh please don't George. It's not worth it. Just ignore him. Please.
GEORGE	*(firmly)* Just one challenge and I won't be responsible.
	(MARJORIE and ERIC appear. They are carrying boxes.)
MARJORIE	Are we the first?
GEORGE	*(jovially)* Hallo there Marje! What you got there – a little snack for Eric? Hallo mate.

(He shakes ERIC'S hand and ERIC nearly drops the box)

MARJORIE This is the ploughmans for the interval. We need to get them all in and put them in the kitchen.

HEATHER Oh I'll help you unload.

(HEATHER disappears out in the direction of the car park. MARJORIE disappears in the opposite direction to the kitchen. ERIC stays chatting to GEORGE.)

ERIC Haven't seen you on the courts much lately George.

GEORGE No, well, I've been a bit busy since I retired, mate. You should try it. Never a spare moment. I've been doing these quizzes all over the place. Did one down at Wallingford last week for a pensioners club.

ERIC Get away.

(MARJORIE comes back and goes towards the exit to the car park to get another box, HEATHER appears with a box and makes for the kitchen.)

MARJORIE *(in a critical tone of voice)* Eric, are you going to stand there all night with that box? We do have a lot to unload you know.

GEORGE Oops. Mustn't hold up the workers. Off you go mate. She-who-must-be-obeyed says you're holding up proceedings.

(ERIC exits to the kitchen)

MARJORIE No George, *you're* the one holding up proceedings. Eric is just easily led.

GEORGE You love me really Marjorie. *(HEATHER appears from the kitchen)* Alright there Heather?

HEATHER Are you going to help unload George?

GEORGE	*(hastily)* I'd best stay here and guard the questions. Don't want some nosy cheat having a quick read before we start.
	(HEATHER looks dubious and goes back into the kitchen. TRACY and MIKE enter, both carrying boxes. TRACY is younger than MIKE and flashy. She likes wearing leopard prints and large earrings. MIKE wears denims and a gloomy expression)
TRACY	*(loudly)* Cooee! Hallo sweety pie!
GEORGE	*(being flirtatious)* It's shapely Tracy! *(They kiss each other on the cheek)* How are your boobs Trace ? Still holding up?
TRACY	*(she giggles)* I see you don't change Georgey Porgy. Here, cop hold of this box and take it into the kitchen, there's a love.
GEORGE	Anything for you luscious. How are you Mike old son? You look knackered – but then what do you expect when you marry a younger woman eh? Eh?
	(MIKE manages a watery smile)
TRACY	Oy! Cheeky! Where's Heather?
GEORGE	In the kitchen, I think. *(To MIKE)* You do look worn out old man. I bet old Tracy's a handful eh?
MIKE	*(unsmiling)* I've been working shifts. I should be in bed really.
TRACY	*(not very sympathetic)* Aah. But I said to him "Get yourself down to the quiz night. Get your brain cells working. It'll be good for you."
MIKE	*(irritated)* I get enough brain activity thank you very much. I need a drink of water.
	(MIKE exits to the kitchen)

TRACY   *(To GEORGE)* Don't take any notice of him love. He's a bit grumpy nowadays. Mid-life crisis I think.

        (HEATHER appears with ERIC. They are talking intimately and sharing a joke.)

GEORGE Oh there you are. Tracy was just asking after you. Eric been having a grope in the kitchen has he?

HEATHER *(flustered)* Oh George, don't be silly.

GEORGE *(expansively to ERIC)* Feel free mate, feel free. *(He dumps his box on HEATHER)* Take that into the kitchen for me will you love?

ERIC   It's alright, let me take it.

GEORGE *(dismissive)* No, she'll do it. Don't pamper her mate, I've got her well trained.

        (HEATHER gives ERIC a look and exits into the kitchen. Meanwhile MARJORIE enters from the car park with three large apple pies covered in cling film and balanced on top of each other.)

MARJORIE I think that's the lot. Eric, would you go to the car and get the spray cream and the large carving knife...ooh, and the serviettes. *(ERIC starts to go)* Eric! You'll need the keys to lock up! *(He comes back and gets the keys then exits).* Hallo Tracy, saw you arriving. Where's Mike gone?

TRACY   Old Misery Guts is out in the kitchen. Tell me George, when are we going to see you in your sexy white shorts playing tennis again?

        (MARJORIE exits to the kitchen, half opens the door and reels back in shock)

MARJORIE   Ooh My God !

TRACY   You alright Marjorie love?

(TRACY goes over to MARJORIE. HEATHER appears quickly from the kitchen looking flustered.)

HEATHER   Marjorie....

MARJORIE   *(embarrassed and unsure what to say)* It's alright. I think I'm just having a hot flush. Don't worry. I'll be fine in a minute.

TRACY   *(Prattling on, oblivious to the look that HEATHER and MARJORIE are giving each other)* Ooh! Have you started getting those? So have I. Bloody nuisance aren't they? I had a terrible hot flush in the middle of Sainsbury's the other day. I felt like taking all my clothes off and plunging into one of the frozen food cabinets!

GEORGE   *(jovially)* Oh let me know next time you go shopping. I'll come and hold your clothes for you!

TRACY   Sauce! *(They both laugh)*

HEATHER   Marjorie...

MARJORIE   *(hissing to her)* How could you? *(louder and rather brisk)* Sorry Heather. I must press on. Speak to you later.

(MARJORIE goes to the kitchen and meets MIKE coming out. They pause for a moment, MIKE looks at the floor, and MARJORIE pushes past him. HEATHER busies herself with GEORGE'S quiz papers. ERIC appears, carrying various items and is followed by an elderly couple SHELAGH and DONALD MACKENZIE. ERIC dumps his bag on the first table).

ERIC	Well our team is here!
GEORGE	Hallo Shelagh, you're looking as lovely as ever.*(He kisses her cheek)* Hallo Donald mate! *(He shakes his hand)*
SHELAGH	We're looking forward to one of your usual stimulating evenings George.
GEORGE	*(conspiratorially)* Sorry Shelagh, we're having a quiz night, I only do the other by personal arrangement!
	(TRACY and ERIC laugh. SHELAGH and DONALD look puzzled)
ERIC	He's being smutty, Shelagh. Don't take any notice. *(ERIC disappears into the kitchen)*
SHELAGH	*(she smiles but still looks bemused)* Oh you'll have to excuse me George. I'm not very quick on the uptake. Shall we select our table Donald?
DONALD	Right here suits me old girl. Close to the gents.
GEORGE	*(trying to be witty)* Prostate playing up is it Donald? *(He laughs)*
DONALD	*(icily)* As a matter of fact it is.
GEORGE	*(looking embarrassed)* Oh no. Sorry. Had the problem long mate?
DONALD	*(smiling)* Oh ages. It'll be a problem for you soon George.
TRACY	Ooh dear. Aren't we getting medical tonight? We've already had the menopause, now it's prostates.
SHELAGH	How awful. Well thankfully I do not have any menopausal problems – not for the last twenty years anyway.
HEATHER	*(putting a Joker on SHELAGH'S table with some feeling. She seems rather miserable.)* Have a Joker.

GEORGE   Oh good, you found them then.

DONALD   *(dryly)* What's this – George's calling card?

HEATHER   *(laughing)* Yes.

GEORGE   *(slightly irritated at being the butt of a joke)* No Donald. The joker system allows you to score double points on any round you nominate with your joker.

DONALD   I see. *(he gets a bottle of wine and some glasses out of a carrier bag)* Wine dear?

SHELAGH   Yes please.

GEORGE   Right. Well we'd better get organised Heather.

                (They go back to their top table. ERIC reappears from the kitchen with DONALD.)

TRACY   Mike, let's sit here.

                (TRACY and MIKE sit down at the table next to DONALD and SHELAGH) I hope Alice and Martin aren't late.

MIKE   They're both coming straight from work. *(Acidly)* People do work you know.

TRACY   *(ignoring MIKE and leaning over to SHELAGH)* How's your daughter getting along?

SHELAGH   Oh very well. She has another baby on the way.

TRACY   How many's that now?

SHELAGH   Three. But a big gap between the other two and this one. Tom and Michael are nine and ten.

DONALD   No. Eleven and ten.

SHELAGH   Are you sure?

DONALD	Yes.
TRACY	Ooh I wouldn't like to start all over again. Not after that sort of gap. Babies are hard work.
MIKE	*(muttering sarcastically)* Not that you would know.
TRACY	*(defensive)* No alright. I know we don't have any. But my sister's got four and they've all been hard work.
	(MARJORIE enters from the kitchen)
MARJORIE	Hallo Shelagh, Hallo Donald. *(She kisses them)* Glad you could come.
SHELAGH	Are you expecting a big turnout?
MARJORIE	I hope so. I've got enough food in the kitchen to feed an army.
GEORGE	*(overhearing)* Who has actually said that they are coming?
MARJORIE	Well, no-one has actually said. But then no-one has actually said that they're not coming. I left it up to them really.
GEORGE	*(concerned)* What advertising did you do?
MARJORIE	Well, the newsletter of course and I made an announcement at the dinner a few weeks ago.
GEORGE	*(aghast)* But we only got our newsletter yesterday! Didn't we Heather?
HEATHER	*(distracted and seemingly unable to look at MARJORIE)* Sorry?
GEORGE	*(getting agitated)* The tennis club newsletter. We only got it yesterday.
HEATHER	Yes, that's right.
GEORGE	*(more agitated)* People won't have had time to make arrangements.

MARJORIE	*(defensively)* But I posted the newsletter two weeks ago.
GEORGE	First class?
MARJORIE	No...
GEORGE	*(exasperated)* Well there you are. Probably half of them haven't even got it yet.
SHELAGH	No dear. We haven't had one. We only knew about this because you asked us to come last week.
MARJORIE	*(realisation dawns)* Oh no! All that food!
HEATHER	Well, there's still ten minutes. They might still turn up.
GEORGE	*(bitterly)* No. No they won't. *(accusingly)* Marjorie, have you any idea how much work goes into preparing a quiz night?
MARJORIE	*(annoyed)* And have you any idea how much effort has gone into preparing all that food!
HEATHER	*(Desperately trying to calm everyone)* Look, don't give up yet. Some people might still come. They might.
	(ALICE, MARTIN and their teenage daughter REBECCA peer nervously around the door)
ALICE	Oh you *are* here! We couldn't see many cars, so we thought we'd got the wrong night!
GEORGE	*(feeling that he has been proved right)* See! I expect lots of people will think there's been a misprint in the newsletter or something. I bet no-one will turn up.
MARJORIE	*(snapping at him)* Oh George, do shut up!
MARTIN	*(cheerily)* Well we've brought an extra one. Come on Rebecca. We couldn't get a babysitter at such short notice.

(A very surly teenage girl follows them in)

REBECCA   *(sullen)* I don't need a babysitter – I'm fourteen.

ALICE   *(firmly)* Let's not go over old ground dear. You'll enjoy it now you're here.

TRACY   Come and join our team! Grab another chair from one of the other tables and sit yourselves down.

GEORGE   *(being very petty)* Well. It's five to. I'll wait until eight o'clock exactly and then I'm going to start.

MARJORIE   *(aggressively)* Fine. Heather, would you help me in the kitchen please?

HEATHER   *(nervously)* Do you really need me?

MARJORIE   *(pointedly)* Oh I think so.

(HEATHER and MARJORIE exit to the kitchen. GEORGE busies himself with his answer sheets. Everyone else opens bottles of wine, pours out drinks and puts crisps and nuts on their tables. There is a sort of lull and everyone murmurs to each other quietly. MARJORIE comes out of the kitchen with a handful of serviettes and pauses in the doorway to say something to HEATHER quietly)

MARJORIE   *(to HEATHER)* All I can say is that I would never have thought it of you. Never in a million years. And nothing you can say will excuse it.

HEATHER   *(looking miserable)* I'm not trying to excuse it.

MARJORIE   *(huffily)* Good. Because you can't.

(MARJORIE marches up to each table and hands serviettes out. She looks cross. HEATHER looks worried. MIKE keeps looking at HEATHER anxiously.)

GEORGE	*(shouting)* RIGHT!
TRACY	Ooh! You made me jump!
	(Everyone falls silent)
GEORGE	*(withering)* Due to a cock-up in communications, it seems that this little gathering is it. The whole quiz night consists of eight people.
MARTIN	Nine.
GEORGE	What?
MARTIN	Nine. We've brought along Rebecca.
GEORGE	*(irritated)* I see. Arguing with me already Martin. Well that's a good start.
MARTIN	I only said...
GEORGE	*(interrupting)* Never mind. I shall run this quiz as though there were fifty people in the room. It makes no difference to me.
MARJORIE	*(losing patience)* Then stop going on about it.
GEORGE	*(ignoring her)* The rules are quite simple. There will be ten rounds of ten questions. Each round will have a different theme.
MARTIN	What are the themes?
GEORGE	I'll come to that in a moment Martin, please. On your tables you will see a large Joker card. You can use it only once because it gives you double points on the round of your choice. I must sec you wave your Joker in the air before the round of your choice, otherwise it will not be accepted. Heather will come round at the end of each round, collect up your papers and do a running score on the

flip chart. And now, in answer to your earlier question, Heather if you would please turn over the chart, you will see the themes for each round.

(HEATHER turns over the flip chart and there is a list of themes as follows :

1.	*Famous People.*
2.	*Islands of the world.*
3.	*Classical music and musicians,*
4.	*Name that advert.*
5.	*Literature.*

INTERVAL FOR REFRESHMENTS

6.	*Food and cookery*
7.	*Timepieces*
8.	*Names and places*
9.	*Cornucopia*
10.	*Kings and Queens of Britain.)*

GEORGE	Any questions?
MARTIN	Yes.
GEORGE	*(sighing)* What a surprise. What is it Martin?
MARTIN	What is Cornucopia?
GEORGE	General Knowledge.
MARTIN	*(being pedantic)* Well why not just say General Knowledge? How are we supposed to know whether to play our Joker if we don't know what the round is about?
GEORGE	*(through gritted teeth)* Well you know now. Will you please

pick a team name.

*(Each table goes into a huddle and debates their name –
except for REBECCA, who is not joining in at all and is
just intent on text-messaging all her friends on her mobile
phone. The debate takes rather too long and GEORGE gets
irritable.)*

GEORGE   Come on! Come on! This is taking far too long!

TRACY   We're ready!

ERIC   So are we.

GEORGE   Well?

TRACY   The Die-hards.

*(HEATHER writes the name on a clean sheet on the
flipchart, draws a line down the centre to create two
columns and waits.)*

ERIC   The Misfits.

(HEATHER writes the name in the other column.)

GEORGE   Right. Let's begin. Does anyone want to play their Joker in
            round one?

(The two tables go into another huddle and debate)

GEORGE   *(getting irritable again)* Oh for goodness sake! We can't do
            this every round. We'll never finish tonight!

TRACY   No.

ERIC   No.

GEORGE   Fine. Question No.1.

MARTIN   Just a minute George…

GEORGE   You can't challenge me already Martin ! I haven't even asked a question yet !

MARTIN   I know that George. It's just that we haven't got any answer
              sheets.

GEORGE   Oh for goodness sake – Heather!

HEATHER   I haven't got them! You've got them!

              *(GEORGE realises that they are in his hand and hastily
              holds them out to HEATHER.)*

GEORGE   For goodness sake!

              *(HEATHER quickly hands them out and returns to the
              flipchart and sits, looking distressed.)*

GEORGE   Right. Famous People. Name the person who said "I have
              nothing to declare but my genius."

              *(Everyone goes into a huddle and seems fairly confident
              that they know the answer. ERIC and TRACY are the
              "writers of the answers" on their respective teams.)*

GEORGE   Question 2. Name the person who said " A hard man is
              good to find".

              (TRACY giggles)

DONALD   Sorry. Could you repeat that?

GEORGE   Yes. Name the person who said "A hard man is good to
              find."

MARTIN   Excuse me.

GEORGE   *(sighing)* Yes Martin. What is it?

MARTIN   *(being pedantic again)* I thought this was a Famous People
              round. All the questions so far have been Quotations.
              Shouldn't this be a Quotations round?

ALICE	Martin, do stop nit-picking.
GEORGE	*(trying to be calm)* No. It's a valid point. But, Martin, as there have only been two questions so far, could you wait until we have done all ten before you leap to criticise?
MARTIN	I just thought I would mention it.
ALICE	Be quiet, there's a dear.
REBECCA	Yeah, Dad. Chill out and let the man ask questions.
MARTIN	*(sarcastically)* Oh – It spoke! Who asked you Miss Mobile Phone? I hope you know that your pocket money is going to pay for the bill on that thing.
MIKE	*(sighing)* It's gonna be a long night.
TRACY	*(turning on MIKE)* Oh don't you start !
MIKE	*(belligerent)* And what does that mean?
TRACY	*(argumentative)* Once you start moaning, you never stop.
MIKE	*(fed up)* Perhaps that's because I have plenty to moan about.
DONALD	*(exasperated)* Can we just get on?
GEORGE	Quite right. Question 3. Name the American philanthropist of the Victorian era who financed cheap housing for the poor of London.
	(Several people suck air through their teeth.)
MARJORIE	That's a tricky one.
MARTIN	*(smugly)* Of course. *(He scribbles a name down on a piece of paper and hands it to TRACY.)*
GEORGE	Question 4. Which famous Edwardian music hall performer was nicknamed "Queen of the Halls?"

ERIC	Haven't you got anything more modern George? I mean I can name all the Spice Girls. *(He laughs)*
REBECCA	*(looking up from her mobile)* They don't exist any more.
DONALD	On second thoughts, Eric, we don't want any questions about pop music. The other side's got Rebecca. They'd win hands down. Wouldn't they love ?
	(REBECCA smiles)
GEORGE	Question 5.
MARJORIE	Hang on a minute! We haven't written down the answer to Question 4.
GEORGE	Well that's your fault.
MARJORIE	*(icily)* Don't get huffy with me George. *(in a threatening tone)* I know things you don't know.
GEORGE	I doubt it.
MARJORIE	*(venomously)* We'll see. *(She pours herself another glass of wine)*
HEATHER	*(nervously)* George, please. Don't speak to Marjorie like that.
GEORGE	Like what?*(firmly)* Question 5. What famous aviator of the early 20th century lost his first child tragically when it was kidnapped and murdered ?
ALICE	*(whispering)* Ooh, ooh, I know – the Murder on the Orient Express thing!
TRACY	The what? *(ALICE whispers in her ear)* Oh, right.
GEORGE	Question 6.
DONALD	You'll have to do without me, team. Nature calls. *(He gets up and heads out the entrance door to the toilets)*

GEORGE	Who was the last British Viceroy of India ?
SHELAGH	Oh, Donald would have known that. Trust him to go and spend a penny when that question came up.
ERIC	Was it the Duke of Windsor ?
MARJORIE	No ! But it was someone royal – I'm sure it was.
SHELAGH	Duke of Kent ?
GEORGE	Question 7.
ERIC	Never mind. We'll go back to it.
GEORGE	Which lady was Queen of England for 11 days?
MARTIN	Hang on a minute !
GEORGE	*(exasperated)* Here we go again.
MARTIN	*(very sure of himself)* No. No. Point of order Mr Questionmaster. Shouldn't this question be in the Kings and Queens round ?
GEORGE	A Queen can still be a famous person can't she?
MARTIN	But if you are going to start mixing up the categories, how can anyone play their Joker properly?
GEORGE	*(coldly)* If you are an expert on Kings and Queens, Martin, there will be plenty of questions in that round for you to play your Joker on.
MARTIN	But all the same...
GEORGE	*(interrupting and getting very shirty)* If I want to put a question about Lady Jane Grey in the famous people's section, I'll sodding well do it !
HEATHER	Martin – you've just given them the answer !
GEORGE	*(appalled)* Oh God ! Now look what you've made me do !

	Just look what you've made me do!
DONALD	*(re-entering and sitting down)* Did I miss anything?
ERIC	Just a barney between Martin and George and George gave away the answer to the question. 'Ere, who was the last British Viceroy of India?
DONALD	Lord Mountbatten.
SHELAGH	I knew he'd know it.
MIKE	*(fed up)* Can we get on? I'm fed up of all this arguing. I could have stayed at home and argued.
TRACY	Yes dear. You do it so well, don't you? *(She laughs half heartedly)*
GEORGE	I'm sorry about that ladies and gentlemen. But I think you will agree I was provoked.
MARTIN	Not by me you weren't.
ALICE and REBECCA	Martin/Dad – shut it!
GEORGE	This will now be a nine-question round. Question 8. What was the name of the architect who designed the Empire State Building?
	(There is a general quiet huddle)
GEORGE	Question 9. What was the name of the captain of the England football team that won the World Cup in 1966?
	(General whispers of "Oh yeah" and "Definitely")
GEORGE	And Question 10. Name the third actor to play James Bond.
MIKE	*(perking up)* I think I might know this one.
MARTIN	So do I. It was Roger Moore.

MIKE	No. That's where you're wrong. It's a trick question. The third actor to play James Bond was David Niven in the spoof movie "Casino Royale".
ALICE	Ooh, I think you're right. How did you know that?
TRACY	*(sharp as a knife)* 'Cos he's the same age as David Niven.
MIKE	Ha bloody ha.
MARTIN	David Niven's dead.
	(Everyone ignores him)
GEORGE	That concludes Round 1. If you would please give your answer sheet to the other team, then we will run through the answers.
	(TRACY hurriedly finishes writing while ERIC stands over her.)
ERIC	Come on. Come on. No cheating now. You're supposed to have stopped writing.
TRACY	Sorry love.
	(She hands over the paper to ERIC and he gives her his paper)
TRACY	*(flirting with ERIC)* A big strong man like you wouldn't hold anything against me, would you?
ERIC	*(entering into the spirit)* I would if given half the chance!
TRACY	Ooh, sailor !
	(ERIC goes back to his seat. MIKE glares at TRACY)
MIKE	Why don't you just give it a rest ?
TRACY	What ?
MIKE	You really fancy yourself don't you ?

TRACY	Well you don't seem to anymore dear – so I have to rely on other admirers.
MIKE	Huh !
	(REBECCA *stares at them both with interest*)
TRACY	(*suddenly aware of REBECCA*) Are you learning from all this dear? Take my advice. Never get yourself hitched up to a miserable old git. It'll make you old before your time.
REBECCA	That's cool. I can see that.
GEORGE	Right. Settle down now. Answer 1. Who said "I have nothing to declare but my genius" – the answer is Oscar Wilde.
ERIC	Oh. We put down Martin Fisher.
MARTIN	(*dryly*) Very funny, Eric. Very flattering.
GEORGE	Answer 2. Who said " A hard man is good to find" – the answer is Mae West.
TRACY	Who?
SHELAGH	Way before your time.
TRACY	Oh.
GEORGE	Answer 3. Name the American philanthropist of the Victorian era who financed cheap housing for the poor of London – the answer is George Peabody.
ERIC	I would have known that if I'd have known what a philan – what he said – was.
MARTIN	(*annoyed*) Actually, I take issue with that.
GEORGE	(*sarcastically*) Oh Martin, what a shame! Did you get one wrong?
MARTIN	No. I put down the right answer. I put Nathaniel Rothschild.

GEORGE	*(firmly)* The answer is George Peabody.
MARTIN	*(standing his ground)* I grant you that George Peabody did build public housing but so did Nathaniel Rothschild.
GEORGE	*(firmly and slowly)* The – answer – is – George – Peabody.

(There is a moment's silence while everyone looks at MARTIN to see how he will respond but MARTIN has decided not to challenge it again and just looks peeved.)

GEORGE	Question 4. Which music hall performer was nicknamed "Queen of the Halls" – the answer is Marie Lloyd.
MARTIN	*(quietly)* I'm sure lots of them had that nickname.
GEORGE	*(overhearing and pouncing on him)* Did you say something Martin?

(MARTIN shakes his head sulkily)

DONALD	*(laughing)* 'Cor – you're having a bad night Martin. That's two you've got wrong.

(MARTIN ignores him)

GEORGE	Question 5. Which famous aviator etc. – The answer was Charles Lindbergh.
TRACY	Well done Alice.
ALICE	*(laughing)* Oh look what they put ! "One of the Wright Brothers"
GEORGE	Question 6. The last British Viceroy of India was Lord Mountbatten.
ERIC	Brilliant Don. Well done mate.
TRACY	You said it was the Duke of Windsor, Martin !
DONALD	He was Governor of the Bahamas mate.

MARTIN	*(sulkily)* I got confused.
GEORGE	Question 7 is null and void.
MARJORIE	Which one was that?
SHELAGH	The Lady Jane Grey one.
GEORGE	Question 8. Architect of the Empire State Building – Frank Lloyd Wright.
ERIC	Yay !
MARJORIE	All down to you Eric. Well done.
GEORGE	Captain of the 1966 England World Cup Team...
EVERYONE	Bobby Moore!
GEORGE	Yes of course. And Question 10. The third actor to play James Bond was David Niven in "Casino Royale".
DONALD, SHELAGH, MARJORIE and ERIC	*(disappointment)* Aaaw !
MARJORIE	I thought it was Roger Moore.
MIKE	*(to his team)* Told you, didn't I?
GEORGE	Heather will now move amongst you, collect the answer sheets and write up the scores.
	(HEATHER does so. Writing up 5 for the Die-hards and 4 for the Misfits)
ERIC	Ooh blimey, team. That's not a very good start is it?
	(DONALD gets up and goes over to MARTIN – enjoying the moment)
DONALD	Not your usual immaculate score, is it Martin?

MARTIN	It is out of nine though, which makes it a little better. Anyway, I disagreed with two of the questions, at least. I mean, if you're going to do these things, you should do them properly.
MIKE	*(trying to wind MARTIN up)* How come you never run quiz nights then Martin? You're always criticising – maybe you could run them properly.
MARTIN	*(making a feeble excuse)* I think my problem would be knowing how to pitch it at a low enough level so that the ordinary person could answer enough of the questions.
DONALD	*(making a face at MIKE)* Yes, we ordinary folk do struggle at these quiz nights don't we?
	(DONALD goes back to his table shaking his head)
ERIC	*(to MARJORIE)* Is that a third glass of wine you're having?
MARJORIE	*(grimly)* It is.
ERIC	Don't you think you'd better take it easy? You've had nothing to eat you know.
MARJORIE	Mind your own business.
ERIC	You're in a funny mood tonight Marje.
MARJORIE	*(matter-of-factly)* I'm not in a funny mood Eric. I'm in a bad mood.
ERIC	Oh don't worry about the lack of turn-out. The Committee will just have to bear the cost of all the left-over food. They can afford it. Flippin' tennis club's rolling in money.
MARJORIE	It's not that.
ERIC	*(desperate)* Then what is it?

MARJORIE	You wouldn't understand.
ERIC	*(resigned)* Oh. That probably means it's my fault.
MARJORIE	For once, Eric, you would be wrong.
ERIC	*(pleading)* So what is it then?
MARJORIE	Never mind.
ERIC	*(shaking his head)* Women.
GEORGE	Right, Let's press on!
DONALD	*(being sensible)* George ! Look, it's taken us three quarters of an hour to do Round 1.
GEORGE	*(looking at MARTIN)* Well I think we know who's fault that is.
DONALD	Well, look, Shelagh and I are getting very hungry. At this rate we'll be eating at midnight. Do you think we could cut out a couple of the rounds ? Make it four rounds per half ?
MIKE	*(relieved)* Yes. Good idea.
GEORGE	*(distressed)* Have you any idea how much work goes into preparing each round? And you want me to just discard a couple of them? Just like that?
DONALD	Oh come on George. I know you work hard - but it won't be wasted, will it? I mean you can recycle them for another quiz night.
GEORGE	*(huffily)* I don't imagine I will be running another quiz night after this one.
MARJORIE	*(slightly drunk and waspish)* Oh George, come on. Don't be childish.
GEORGE	I beg your pardon?

ERIC	*(hastily)* Look old man, I know nothing about geography and I don't imagine anyone else does…
MARTIN	Speak for yourself.
ERIC	…so this next round "Islands of the World" would probably be a waste of time. We'd get really miserable scores and it wouldn't be worth your while…
MARTIN	I wouldn't get a miserable score!
ALICE	Oh Martin do shut up!
DONALD	*(standing up in annoyance)* Yes. Give it a rest Martin. You're not as clever as you think you are.
MARTIN	*(also standing up)* How dare you!
MIKE	Sit down both of you! This is just holding things up more.
GEORGE	*(self-pitying)* Well I'm sorry if you think this is all a waste of time…
TRACY	Nobody's saying that…
SHELAGH	I'm enjoying it George.
ERIC	*(raising his voice)* It's just that we're all hungry!
MARJORIE	*(losing her temper with ERIC)* Will you stop going on about your bloody stomach !
MIKE	Don't shout at the poor bloke, Marjorie…
MARJORIE	*(shouting louder)* Don't you speak to me like that – not after what I know about you…
TRACY	*(aggressive and suspicious)* What does she mean? *(raising her voice and advancing on MARJORIE)* What do you mean?
HEATHER	*(desperate)* George, stop them !

GEORGE	*(shouting really loudly)* THAT'S ENOUGH! You're behaving like children!
	(Suddenly an elderly woman and a girl come in through the door. There is an embarrassed silence and they all stare at the newcomers)
GEORGE	*(suddenly affable)* Yes? Can I help you?
PAT	Is this the quiz night?
GEORGE	Yes.
PAT	Sorry we're so late but my granddaughter received a text message from her friend to say that you needed more members. Can we join in?
REBECCA	*(waving)* Hi Sally! I'm here!
ALICE	*(craning to have a look)* I'm sure I know that woman.
PAT	I'm Pat Pendleton and this is my granddaughter Sally. Have we missed much?
GEORGE	No. Only one round actually.
PAT	Oh? I thought you'd be well advanced by now. I said to Sally, we might not be able to join in, we're so late.
GEORGE	Oh no, no, no. It's only a friendly quiz night you know. As you can see there aren't many of us here. Just a…um… happy little band of friends. We…er…got held up but we're going to make up the time. We're going to cut out a couple of rounds to speed things up. Why don't you sit at that table over there?
REBECCA	*(getting up)* Can I join your team Mrs Pendleton? I'm spare on this team.
PAT	Oh are you Sally's friend? That would be nice.

(PAT, SALLY and REBECCA sit down at a spare table)

ALICE   *(hissing)* I know who she is now – Mrs Pendleton – don't
               you remember Martin ?

MARTIN   No.

ALICE   She was our history teacher at school! I didn't know she
               was still around! Eric, you went to our school, do you
               remember Mrs Pendleton? Was she there when you were there?

ERIC   Crikey! Yes she was! A bit of a dragon too!

ALICE   Oh she wasn't! She was better than some.

ERIC   True. But she didn't stand any nonsense did she?

MARTIN   *(loudly to GEORGE)* We haven't decided which round to
               cut out of the second half. Can I suggest Kings and Queens
               of Britain?

ALICE   *(shocked)* Martin !

MARTIN   *(whispering to Alice)* Well, she's a history teacher – she'll
               walk that one.

DONALD   *(annoyed)* Oy, I'm quite up on Kings and Queens. I vote we
               get rid of Timepieces. I know bugger all about clocks.

ERIC   Yeah. I'm with you mate.

GEORGE   Can we have a vote? Who wants to drop Kings and Queens?
               (MARTIN and TRACY put their hands up)
               Who wants to drop Timepieces?
               (Everyone else puts their hands up, including the new team)
               Right. So we'll whizz through the next three rounds so that
               we can all eat. OK?

PAT   Sorry. What round have you cut out of this section?

GEORGE   Oh. Islands of the World.

PAT	Oh that's a shame. I'm quite good at geography.
MARTIN	*(sulkily)* What else is she good at?
ALICE	Oh don't be petty Martin. She's all on her own with two teenagers. I'm sure they haven't got any special advantage. *(MARTIN looks doubtful)*
GEORGE	Right. Eyes down and ears open for the next round. Classical music and musicians.
	(A collective groan goes up. GEORGE presses a button and the first few bars of Beethoven's Fifth boom out.)

BLACKOUT

END OF SCENE 1

MIXED DOUBLES
SCENE 2

It is at the end of the supper break. There are paper plates with the remains of ploughmans on and some people are still eating their apple pie with spray cream. MARJORIE is circulating with some uneaten ploughmans, trying to persuade more people to eat them. GEORGE is eating alone up at his quiz-master's table. HEATHER is writing in the team scores from the round before the break. It appears that the new team is called "The Schoolyard" and they are already way ahead. "The Misfits" have 20, "The Die-hards" have 24 and "The Schoolyard" have 27. MARTIN is looking sulky. TRACY and MIKE are not speaking. ALICE is gathering up the debris into a black sack. DONALD is in the toilet. SHELAGH and ERIC are having a quiet talk. The two teenagers are playing electronic games on their mobile phones. PAT is still eating.

MARJORIE	Come along now. Surely someone wants another ploughmans ?
ERIC	I've already had three!
MARJORIE	What about you Martin?
MARTIN	I'm not hungry.
MARJORIE	Mike? *(acidly)* I know that you've been busy working up an appetite.
MIKE	No thanks.
	(MARJORIE goes off into the kitchen in a huff)
TRACY	*(suspicious again)* What did she mean by that ?
MIKE	Nothing. Ignore her.
TRACY	She keeps having a pop at you. Have you upset her?

MIKE	I never have anything to do with the woman!
TRACY	I wouldn't be surprised if you've upset her. You're not exactly Mr Tact are you.
MIKE	*(sarcastically)* Oh you know everything, don't you.
	(They both go back to ignoring each other. ALICE, by this time has reached PAT'S table and decides to try and be nauseatingly friendly.)
ALICE	Hello Mrs Pendleton ! I don't suppose you remember me, do you? Alice Potter....I was in your class a very long time ago.
PAT	Of course I remember you Alice. History wasn't your strong point but I remember you as a diligent child.
ALICE	*(unsure of the meaning of diligent)* Oh, I'm sure I wasn't as bad as all that. *(laughing nervously)*
REBECCA	*(sighing)* She means you worked hard, mum.
ALICE	*(embarrassed)* I know that! I was only joking.
PAT	And I particularly remember your husband, Martin. Still knows everything does he?
REBECCA	Oh cool, Mrs P. You really did know my dad, didn't you?
ALICE	Rebecca! Don't be so disrespectful! You should call Mrs Pendleton by her full name!
PAT	It's alright, I like being called Mrs P.
ALICE	Oh, well then, Mrs P...
PAT	*(firmly)* Only by Rebecca, dear. I think you should stick to Mrs Pendleton.
ALICE	*(wishing the floor would open up)* Right. Of course....well

I'd..er…better get on then. It's so nice to see you again Mrs Pendleton. *(She makes a swift exit to the kitchen)*

SALLY   Gran. That wasn't kind, was it ?

PAT   I'm too old to be kind any more dear. I spent forty years as a teacher, smiling and being kind. It made my face ache. I've given all that up.

(GEORGE comes over – being the affable host)

GEORGE   I'm so glad you were able to come, Pat. It's nice to have some fresh faces at these things.

PAT   Well, I'm hardly fresh, but my two team mates are. Very bright girls – both of them.

GEORGE   Oh yes. I've known Rebecca since she was a toddler. She's always impressed me. What did you say this young ladies' name was?

SALLY   *(confidently, holding out her hand, which rather unnerves GEORGE)* I'm Sally, how do you do?

GEORGE   *(shaking her hand reluctantly)* Er…Sally…yes. *(To PAT)* Young people eh?

PAT   Are you always the quiz-master?

GEORGE   To tell you the truth, the tennis club don't have a quiz night very often, the people here…well…they're not the intellectual type you know… but I run lots of others, all over the place. It's my main hobby since I retired.

PAT   Really? We must discuss the possibility of you running a quiz night sometime for The Retired Teachers Association.

GEORGE   *(positively glowing)* Retired Teachers? Marvellous! Anytime, Pat, anytime. Just say the word. Well I'd better go and prepare for the second half.

(GEORGE goes back to the top table)

SALLY   I didn't know there was a Retired Teachers' Association, Gran.

PAT   Yes, well, I just wonder if they'll thank me. I shouldn't have opened my mouth really - I didn't think. Silly of me really.

SALLY   He seems alright.

PAT   *(pulling a face)* I'm not so sure.

(Everyone engages in mimed conversation on their tables. GEORGE turns to HEATHER who is busying herself gathering up the answer sheets.)

GEORGE   *(happy)* That's the sort of calibre of person I like to deal with at quiz nights. Someone with brains and education. Makes it all worthwhile. Makes it more of a challenge.

HEATHER   Who are you talking about dear ?

GEORGE   That Pat Pendleton. Very impressive mind that woman. Very impressive. You'd better hand out some more answer sheets. Eric's team have spoiled two of theirs by spilling red wine over them.

HEATHER   Yes George. *(She hands out answer sheets to the tables – MARTIN'S team first, then ERIC's. As she is on her way to PAT's team, MIKE gets up and goes to talk to her)*

MIKE   Has Marjorie spoken to you?

HEATHER   *(nervously)* Yes she has. She's not very happy I can tell you. I'm so worried that she's going to tell George.

MIKE   Why would she do that?

HEATHER	I don't know. She's very friendly with George. They're on two Committees together, you know.
MIKE	I don't know what it's got to do with her. She keeps making snide remarks to me.
HEATHER	I'd better get on. Marjorie's come back.
	(ALICE and MARJORIE have come out of the kitchen and are talking quietly in the doorway. HEATHER and MIKE separate. MIKE goes back to his seat, HEATHER gives PAT's table some sheets and goes back to the top table.)
GEORGE	*(raising his voice)* Right. Now. Let's start the second half shall we?
DONALD	I just have to go to the toilet mate.
GEORGE	Donald! You should have gone in the interval.
DONALD	I did. *(He exits)*
SHELAGH	He shouldn't drink wine really.
GEORGE	Let's start anyway. I see that The Schoolyard have forged ahead, even though they have only competed in three rounds to everyone else's four. However, there is still time for the other teams to pass them. Eyes down everyone for the Food and Cookery round.
ERIC	Marjorie should be good at this one.
MARJORIE	*(still in a bad mood)* Don't try and ingratiate yourself with me Eric.
ERIC	*(totally stumped)* What have I done now?
GEORGE	Question 1. What shape is the pasta called "conchiglie"? Heather will write the spelling of this on the flip chart.

(HEATHER does so. There is a pause while everyone writes things down silently and whispers to each other)

GEORGE   Question 2. What is "focaccia"? Heather will write down the spelling for you again.

(HEATHER does so again)

MARTIN   Excuse me.

(There is a collective groan from everyone except The Schoolyard table)

MARTIN   I just wondered if all the questions are about Italian food.

GEORGE   Does it matter? *(MARTIN does not answer)* Well – does it?

MARTIN   No. I suppose not.

GEORGE   Question 3. Where in the world would you expect to find laverbread on the table? And if you say, Italy, Martin, you would be wrong.

(DONALD comes back at this point. He looks at the board. HEATHER is writing "laverbread".)

DONALD   *(cheerily)* Do you know – I had every one of those for lunch today.

ERIC   You didn't!

DONALD   Cross my heart. I had con – watsit, I'm not even going to attempt the other word ' cos there are ladies present and that bread in my soup.

SHELAGH   Oh Donald, you are a silly sod.

GEORGE   Question 4. Where in the world would you eat a dish called "tempura"? Heather, please...

(She writes the word on the flip chart again)

TRACY	Why in the world would you want to?
ERIC	Your lovely assistant is working well tonight George! She's got a very sensuous movement with that felt tip pen.
MARJORIE	*(very ratty)* Be quiet Eric!
GEORGE	Question 5. What is couscous made from? Heather...once more please...
	(HEATHER writes the word)
MIKE	*(grumpily)* I don't suppose there is a question about bacon, egg and chips, is there?
TRACY	*(irritated)* God you are miserable tonight. *(MIKE glares at her)*
GEORGE	Question 6. What is the principal ingredient of "hummus".
	(HEATHER writes the word)
MARTIN	You don't spell it like that.
GEORGE	*(seamlessly)* Write the alternative spelling dear.
	(HEATHER writes "houmous" on the chart)
GEORGE	Question 7.
ERIC	Hang on a minute George. You're speeding up!
GEORGE	How are the Schoolyard doing? Am I too fast for you Pat?
PAT	No we're fine, aren't we girls?
SALLY	No probs.
REBECCA	Yep.
GEORGE	You just have to keep up Eric.
MARJORIE	*(slurring her words slightly)* Please don't speak to Eric like that George.

(GEORGE ignores her.)

GEORGE	Question 7. What are blinis?

(HEATHER writes the word without being asked. SALLY and REBECCA whoop with delight. Everyone turns round)

PAT	Sorry. It's just that they made blinis in school today.
ALICE	Really!? In my day all we ever made was rice pudding or shepherds pie!
REBECCA	We do sophisticated multi-cultural cuisine now, Mum.
MARTIN	*(venomously to ALICE)* And you said old Pendleton wouldn't have much of an advantage because she was all on her own with two teenagers.
ALICE	Shh! She'll hear you.
GEORGE	Question 8. What ingredient makes Thai Fragrant rice, fragrant ?
ERIC	Bloody hell George! What is tie fragrant rice?
GEORGE	Fragrant, that is, perfumed, rice from Thailand.
MARJORIE	*(loudly)* He knows what fragrant means! He's not that stupid!
ERIC	*(worried)* Don't drink any more Marje. You're getting very aggressive.
MARJORIE	Shut up!
GEORGE	I didn't say Eric was stupid. I was merely explaining.
DONALD	Sorry, what was the question again?
TRACY	What makes fragrant rice, fragrant.
GEORGE	Thank you Tracy.

(There are general mutterings)

SALLY	*(To PAT and REBECCA)* We should have played our joker on this round.
REBECCA	Too right. I'll laugh if the next question is about Mexican food.
PAT	Why?
SALLY	We've just spent the last two weeks doing it for a special project.
GEORGE	Question 9. What is a tortilla ?
	(HEATHER writes it on the chart)
SALLY AND REBECCA	*(shrieking)* Wicked!
GEORGE	More multicultural cuisine at school?
PAT	*(smiling)* I'm afraid so.
MARTIN	*(sulking)* Oh this is ridiculous!
GEORGE	And finally, Question 10. What is Welsh Rarebit ?
	(ERIC'S team cheer)
DONALD	Finally – something we've heard of!
GEORGE	That concludes the round on Food and Cookery. If you would please finish writing, then pass your answer sheets to the team on your immediate right, as before.
ALICE	I think I'd better mark The Schoolyard's paper this time, Martin. You only get yourself in a state when they get them all right.
MARTIN	Don't be so silly.
TRACY	She's right. You do. You musn't take it so seriously Martin. My God, Alice, why couldn't we have been in a team with

men who have a bit of a laugh? Instead of being stuck with Mr Misery Guts and Mr Neurotic.

(Both MIKE and MARTIN turn away and sulk. TRACY passes their paper to ERIC. DONALD passes their paper to PAT. REBECCA passes her paper to ALICE)

GEORGE   Right. Are we ready? Question 1. The pasta called conchiglie is in the shape of a conch shell.

SHELAGH   Will you accept shell ?

GEORGE   No I'm afraid not. I mean there are all types of shells aren't there ?

MARTIN   I might have known he'd be pedantic.

GEORGE   *(smugly)* It's a question of standards Martin. Question 2. Focaccia is a type of Italian flat bread made with olive oil.

MARJORIE   And herbs.

GEORGE   No. Just olive oil.

MARJORIE   *(aggressively)* I make it all the time and it contains herbs.

GEORGE   Well, I'll have to consult my expert here. Heather compiled the food round. Heather, does focaccia contain herbs?

(HEATHER looks reluctant to answer)

HEATHER   Well….not according to The Magic of Italy….

MARJORIE   *(exploding)* I don't care what any bloody book says! I've been making it for ten years and I've always used herbs!

ERIC   Steady on Marjorie.

GEORGE   I'm afraid I must defer to Heather on this.

MARJORIE   *(in a rage)* Oh must you! Why? Because Heather is so perfect? Well she's not!

GEORGE	*(alarmed)* Marjorie!
MARJORIE	*(bitter)* You're always ramming down my throat what a perfect wife Heather is – what a lovely woman – what an intelligent person. You're a fool George – a complete bloody fool! She *(she points at HEATHER)* is having an affair with him! *(pointing at the next table)* I saw them kissing in the kitchen !
ALICE	*(misunderstanding and horrified)* Martin!?
REBECCA	*(also horrified)* Dad!?
MARJORIE	*(exasperated)* No not him – him! *(She points directly at MIKE)*
TRACY	*(astounded)* Mike!?
HEATHER	Oh my God.
MIKE	*(standing up and moving to one side, motioning HEATHER to join him)* Well, now that it's out in the open, we might as well own up.
	(HEATHER scurries across and holds hands with MIKE, smiling bravely at him)
TRACY	I don't believe this! You've been carrying on behind my back with a woman who's twenty years *older* than me!? What is the attraction?
MIKE	We have a lot in common. We're the same age. We like the same things. We remember the same things.
TRACY	So what does that mean? You sit round and swap Vera Lynn photos or something?
MIKE	You wouldn't understand.
TRACY	Try me. I can get my head round nostalgia.

HEATHER	*(feeling brave)* We go to Sixties' revival concerts.
MIKE	Brian Poole and the Tremeloes – Freddie and the Dreamers… *(MIKE and HEATHER smile at each other)*
HEATHER	The Hollies.
GEORGE	*(finding his voice)* The Hollies! But you've always listened to Radio Three!
HEATHER	No George. *You've* always listened to Radio Three. When you go out I always put on Capital Gold.
TRACY	*(shaking her head in disbelief)* Fine. So apart from the trips down Memory Lane, what else, exactly do you see in my husband?
HEATHER	*(taking a deep breath and smiling)* He makes me laugh.
TRACY	*(beside herself)* He WHAT! ! *(to everyone else)* He makes her laugh!!!!……… Do you know what I've had to put up with for the last fifteen years – do you? I used to be laugh- a-minute Tracy before I married this miserable git! People used to say " Here comes Tracy – like a little ray of sunshine is Tracy". I used to be popular – invited to all the parties. Then I married that miserable sod. Everyone – *everyone* warned me against him but I wouldn't listen. I was twenty-five and in love with an older man. He could do no wrong in my eyes. But he turned out to be so miserable, all my friends stopped inviting me to parties. I just had to sit at home and listen to him moaning about his bad back, his feet, his pay packet and every other bloody thing in the world. *(Turning back to MIKE and HEATHER and trying to be calm)* I don't mind you having an affair with him – you're welcome to him. *(She starts getting hysterical)* It's the

fact that I get all the black looks and the sulks and the showing off and you get Coco the Bloody Clown! *(She collapses into her chair sobbing)*

MIKE   We never meant anyone to get hurt. No-one would have known but for that malicious cow. Why she had to interfere I don't know.

GEORGE   *(finding his voice again and turning to MARJORIE)* Yes. Why did you interfere?

MARJORIE   I'll tell you why George. Because when I offered you my...my heart...my friendship. When I wanted us to be more than friends – you turned me down...because you said you couldn't do that to Heather, who was so loyal, so faithful...you turned me down.

ERIC   *(shocked)* Marjorie!? You...and...George?

MARJORIE   I just told you didn't I? Nothing happened. He didn't want to!

ERIC   But why?

MARJORIE   Oh for God's sake Eric...you're always so flippant about everything. Always having a laugh and a joke. George... takes things seriously. I like that in a man. Seriousness.

MARTIN   *(loudly)* I don't believe this. One is fed up with her husband because he doesn't laugh and the other one is fed up because he does.

ERIC   *(completely flipping)* You shut your mouth! I've had enough of you...you *(Leaping at MARTIN and grabbing him by the throat)* bloody little know-it- all! *(ALICE and TRACY scream, MARTIN and ERIC scuffle.)*

TRACY   *(Turning on MIKE and hitting him repeatedly with her handbag)* I could kill you as well!

(Pandemonium breaks out. HEATHER tries to stop TRACY, GEORGE tries to stop ERIC. Suddenly there is a long blast on a whistle, being blown by PAT, who has walked up to the top table. She has gone into Automated Teacher Mode. Everyone stops what they are doing and, when there is silence, she stops blowing the whistle.)

PAT   *(speaking calmly but with great authority)* Absolutely disgraceful behaviour. Stand by your chairs, all of you.

(There is a pause while everyone looks uncertain about what to do. She raises her voice with great authority.)

I said immediately !

(Everyone shuffles around frantically trying to stand behind their chair. Those who are still seated, stand up behind their chairs. There is a farcical moment where GEORGE and HEATHER cannot get to the top table so they go and stand behind two chairs on an empty table.)

PAT   That's better. I will not tolerate fighting. *(turning to ERIC)* Eric Smith, you were always too ready to use brute force in the playground, as far as I remember. *(turning to MARTIN)* And as for you, Martin Fisher, that mouth of yours was always getting you into trouble. Always voicing your opinion and winding the others up. *(GEORGE sniggers)* Do you find something funny, George? *(His amusement disappears and he shakes his head)* I should think not. I do not find this situation amusing at all.

Eric and Martin, shake hands and apologise please. *(They look reluctant. She snaps at them)* AT ONCE!

(ERIC and MARTIN shake hands reluctantly and mumble "Sorry" half-heartedly) Now you can all sit down quietly.

(They do so. DONALD puts his hand up) Yes ?

DONALD	Please may I go to the toilet?
PAT	You may. *(He exits)* Now I suggest you gather up all your belongings, making sure that you don't leave anything behind please, and vacate the building in an orderly fashion.
ALICE	Shall I...
PAT	No speaking please Alice.
ALICE	But..
PAT	*(glaring at her)* No speaking!

(Everyone silently gathers up their carrier bags and handbags and begins to file out. ERIC decides to get masterful and bundles a dejected and drunken MARJORIE out of the door. PAT goes back to her table.)

SALLY	Jeez, Gran. You were awesome!
PAT	Was I dear? Well I'm shaking like a leaf – but don't tell anyone.

(TRACY, MIKE, HEATHER and GEORGE linger. They all look at each other, then MIKE takes HEATHER'S hand and they stand together.)

TRACY	Good riddance. *(She storms out)*

(GEORGE looks at HEATHER.)

HEATHER	I'll come and get my things tomorrow George.
GEORGE	So it's final is it ?
HEATHER	Yes.

(HEATHER and MIKE leave. PAT goes up to GEORGE)

PAT	Thank you very much George for all the hard work you did. I'm sorry it didn't work out.
REBECCA	Thanks.
SALLY	Yeah. Thanks.
GEORGE	I suppose you've reconsidered the Retired Teachers Association quiz now.
PAT	I think it's best. Goodnight. *(PAT, SALLY and REBECCA leave)*

(There is a long pause while GEORGE slowly packs his stuff away – then he turns to the audience and speaks out loud to himself)

GEORGE   Who's going to do my running totals now?

(There is a brief moment where we can see the pain and confusion on his face then BLACKOUT and MUSIC)

THE END

FURNITURE LIST

Throughout: four small tables (card table size); four chairs around each table; small "top table" (if room) for the quizmaster (otherwise just a chair); two chairs for GEORGE and HEATHER; flipchart on a stand with a score sheet drawn up and a list of categories on the sheet underneath.

Set dressing : tennis club notice board; perhaps some posters for racquets or tennis shoes; small posters or notices about matches.

PROPERTY LIST

NOTE : everyone needs to have half-eaten paper plates of food in their bags to put on the tables during the blackout.

Page 1:	GEORGE : sets up CD player. HEATHER : large bag; score sheets; Jokers; pens etc.
Page 2:	MARJORIE : box of food, handbag. ERIC : box of food.
Page 3:	HEATHER : box of food.
Page 4:	TRACY: box of food; handbag; bag with wine, 2 glasses and crisps. MIKE: box of food.
Page 5:	MARJORIE: three large apple pies covered in cling film; car keys.
Page 6:	ERIC: can of spray cream; carving knife; large packet of serviettes, bag with wine, 2 glasses and nibbles. SHELAGH: handbag. DONALD: bag with wine, mineral water, 2 glasses and nibbles.
Page 7:	HEATHER: puts a Joker on SHELAGH's table.
Page 10:	ALICE: handbag. MARTIN: carrier bag with wine, Coca Cola, 3 glasses and nibbles. REBECCA: mobile phone.
Page 11:	MARJORIE: brings on a handful of serviettes from the kitchen.

Page 15:   GEORGE: needs to have the answer sheets in his hand
                for HEATHER to hand out.

Page 27:   PAT: carrier bag with soft drinks, glasses and crisps.
                Whistle in her pocket.
                SALLY: mobile phone.

Page 30:   EVERYONE: See NOTE at start of list.
                ALICE: black plastic sack to put rubbish in.
                SALLY: playing game on mobile phone.
                REBECCA: playing game on mobile phone.
                MARJORIE: circulating with uneaten ploughman's
                covered in cling film.

Page 33:   HEATHER hands out more answer sheets.

Page 42:   TRACY: repeatedly hits MIKE with her handbag.

Page 43:   PAT: blows her whistle.

LIGHTING PLOT

To open: *general interior lighting.*

Page 29:   cue: first few bars of Beethoven's Fifth.
                  Blackout.

Page 30:   *raise lights again after agreed period.*

Page 45   cue: GEORGE: "Who's going to do my running totals
                  now?"
                  Blackout.

EFFECTS PLOT

To open: introductory music.

Page 29:   cue: GEORGE: "Classical music and musicians"
                  *Play the opening few bars of Beethoven's Fifth which can
                  either carry on throughout the blackout or be replaced by a
                  "passing time" effect, such as a ticking clock (or the
                  COUNTDOWN theme).*

Page 45:   cue: GEORGE: "Who's going to do my running totals
                  now?"
                  Heartbeat pause, blackout and closing music.